JULES

and Nina

dine out

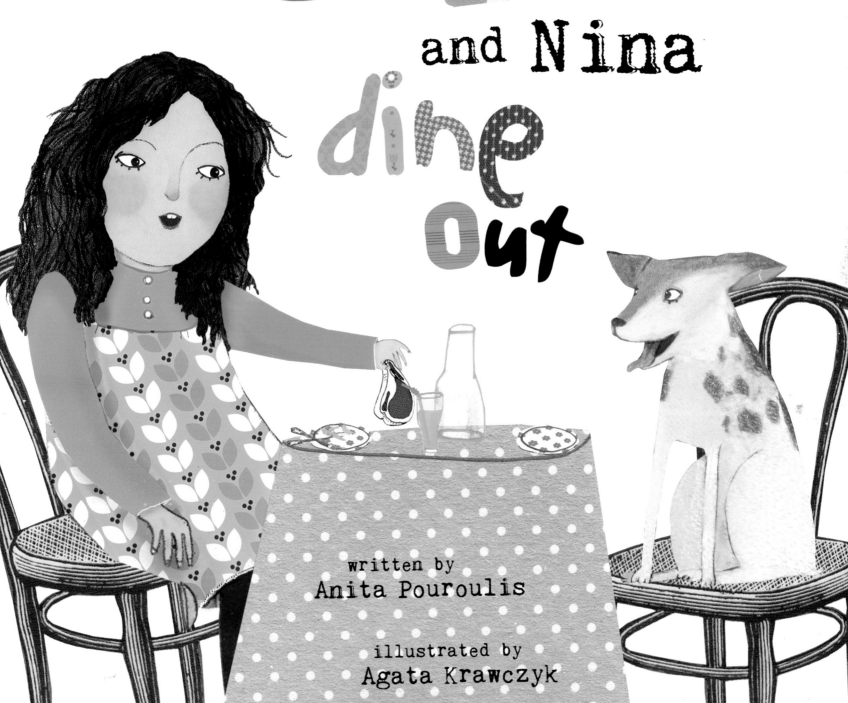

written by
Anita Pouroulis

illustrated by
Agata Krawczyk

AP - For the other AP,

who always believes in me

AK - For Staś

Hi, I'm **Jules**!
These are my dogs,
Nina and **George**.

Mum feels Nina is a **totally spoilt** dog who thinks she's a human being.

Dad says any **normal** dog would be happy **gnawing** on a **bone** in the garden.

Once upon a time, things were different.
Both Nina and George used to come out with us.

But now George **doesn't** join us for lunch. Or dinner. Or **breakfast**.

Not since that time George
got his teeth around
a big, **juicy steak.**

It was a steak that did **not**
belong to George,
but to someone who
was **enjoying** her lunch
until George
came along.

Nina sits very **quietly** under the table when we go out.

She loves it there, especially when I d r o p scraps of food onto the floor by mistake.

My parents don't like Nina eating everything that comes her way.

Mum always moans,

"Don't give her that! She'll get gas and then things will get smelly!"

Anyway,
    you won't believe what happens
        when we arrive at the restaurant today!

    The restaurant manager inspects Nina.

He takes a good look at her
                and **shakes** his head.

"**Erm!** Four-legged
        creatures
    are **not** allowed
inside this restaurant!"
    he splutters.

Come in
WE'RE
OPEN

I argue that Nina has been to **more** restaurants than she could even count on her paws.

But the manager will **absolutely** **not** change his mind.

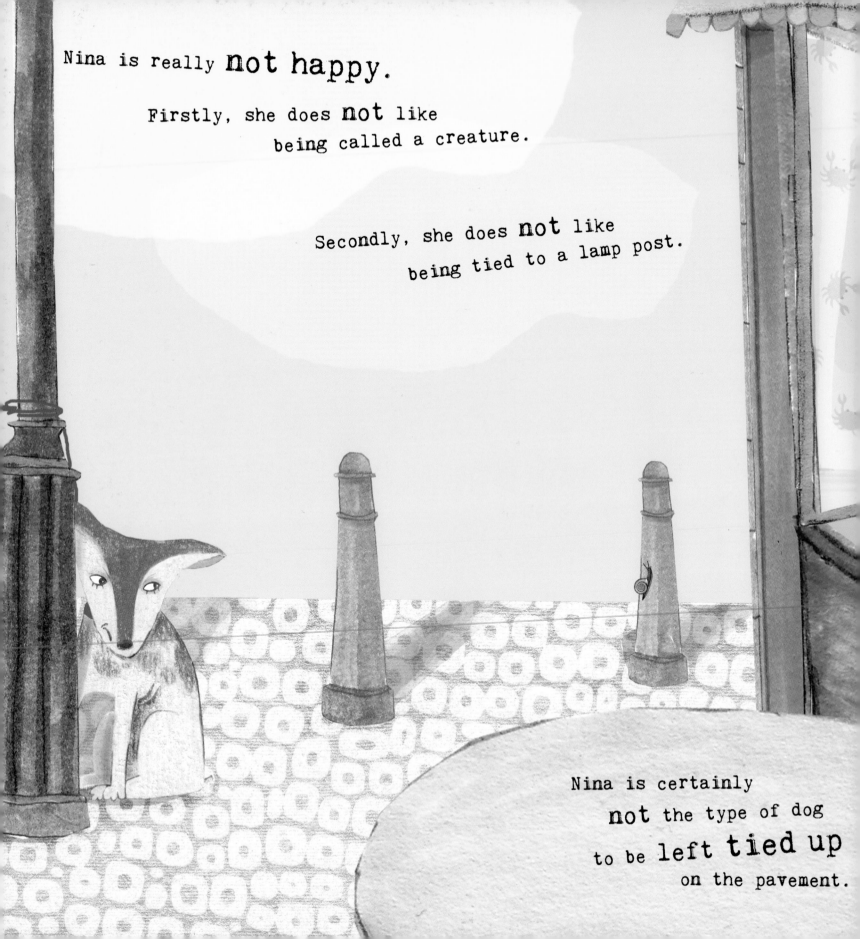

Nina is really **not happy.**

Firstly, she does **not** like
being called a creature.

Secondly, she does **not** like
being tied to a lamp post.

Nina is certainly
not the type of dog
to be **left tied up**
on the pavement.

We sit by the window
to keep an eye on Nina.

Mum says, "Never mind,
Nina can have a good
nap in the sun!"

Dad mutters,
"I told you dogs
belong in the yard
at home."

I wonder what Nina
would be saying
right NOW if she could talk...

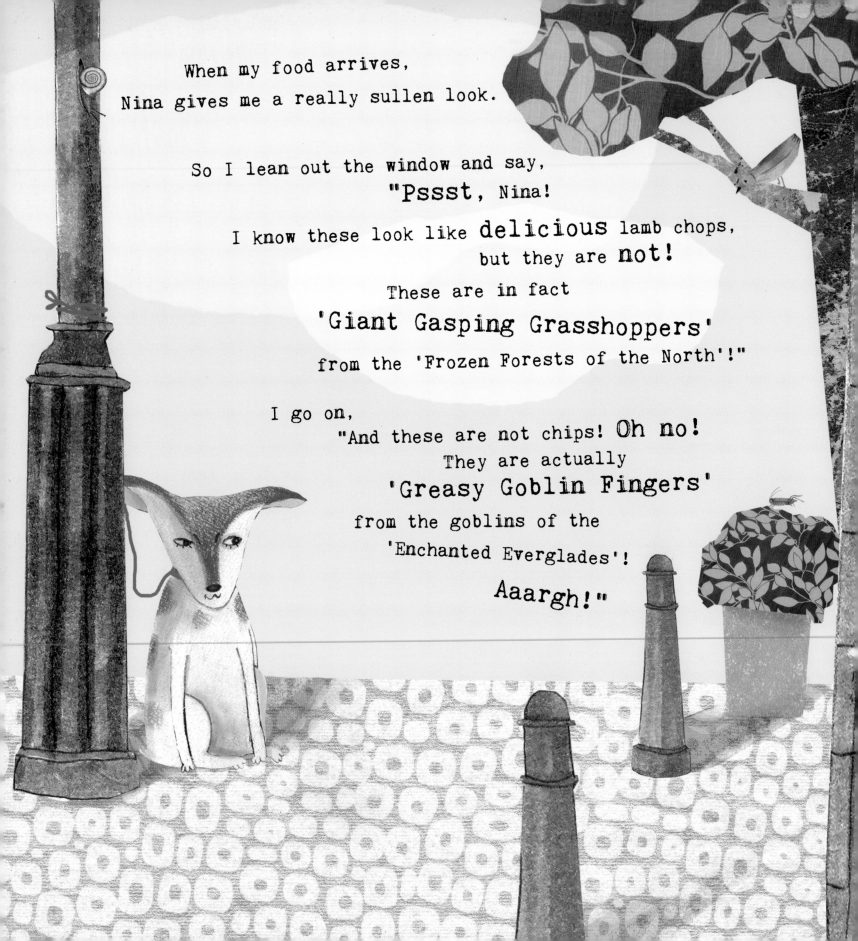

When my food arrives,
Nina gives me a really sullen look.

So I lean out the window and say,
"Pssst, Nina!

I know these look like delicious lamb chops,
but they are not!
These are in fact
'Giant Gasping Grasshoppers'
from the 'Frozen Forests of the North'!"

I go on,
"And these are not chips! Oh no!
They are actually
'Greasy Goblin Fingers'
from the goblins of the
'Enchanted Everglades'!

Aaargh!"

"And this isn't tomato sauce…"
I say.

"It's actually a sticky red goo
that oozes from the skin of the
'Larruping Lizards',
so they can slide along
the hard rocks in 'Vicious Valley'!

All of this horrible stuff
is supposed to be good
for growing children!"

Mum and Dad are **not** impressed.

"**Keep** your **voice down**, Jules.
People will hear you!"

says Mum,
looking aggravated.

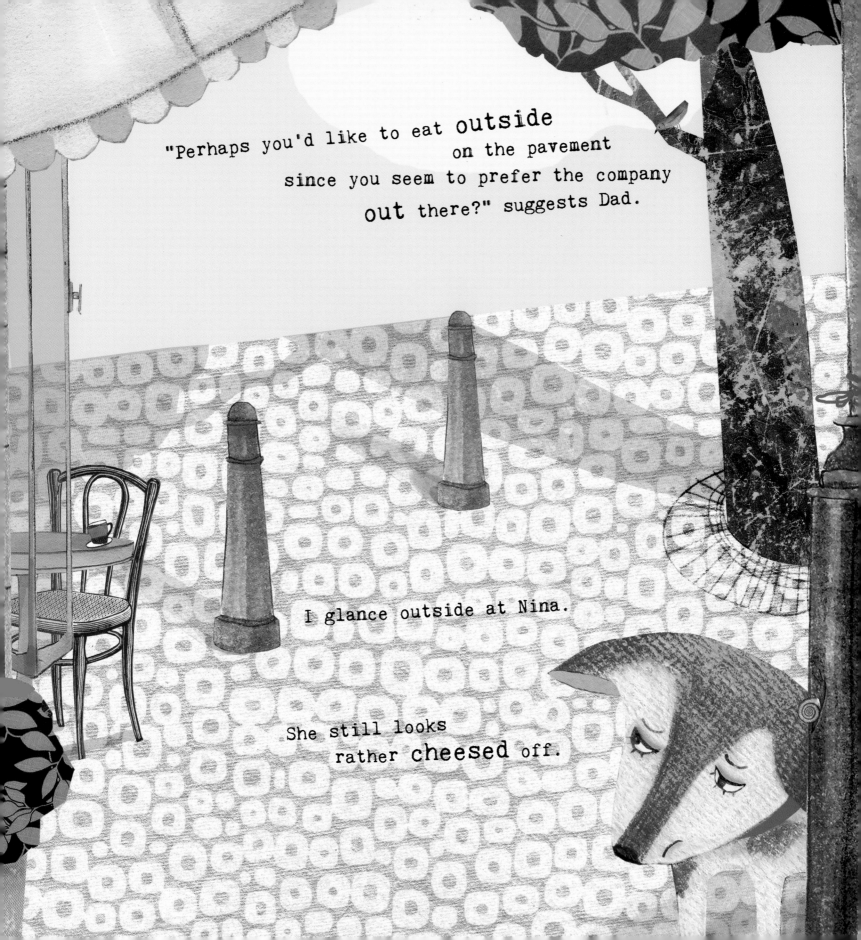

"Perhaps you'd like to eat outside on the pavement since you seem to prefer the company out there?" suggests Dad.

I glance outside at Nina.

She still looks rather cheesed off.

When pudding arrives,
I call to Nina,

"Psst, Nina!
You think this is chocolate cake?
Well, think again!
It's really a scrunch of
'Scraggly Snails'
who hide in the
'Wicked Waters of the West'!
And these cherries
are actually the

'Elephantine Eyeballs
of the Red-Eyed
Terrible Toads'
who live there too!"

"Uuuuuurgh!"
I roll my eyes
and stick my
my tongue
out.

Nina looks at me.

She looks as horrified as a dog can look.

The manager looks at me.

He looks as horrified as a restaurant manager can look.

A moment later
the manager is back
with two wrapped packages
in his hands.

"Here's your cake,
young lady.

And this one has leftovers
for your dog,"
he says.

I show the parcels to Nina
as we collect her from the lamp post.

"You see!" I tell her excitedly,
"you're going to have
lunch after all!"

Nina looks at me
like I'm the strangest person
who ever lived on this earth.

When we get home

George is there

to greet us.

I call,
"Here, boy!"
and open the leftovers.

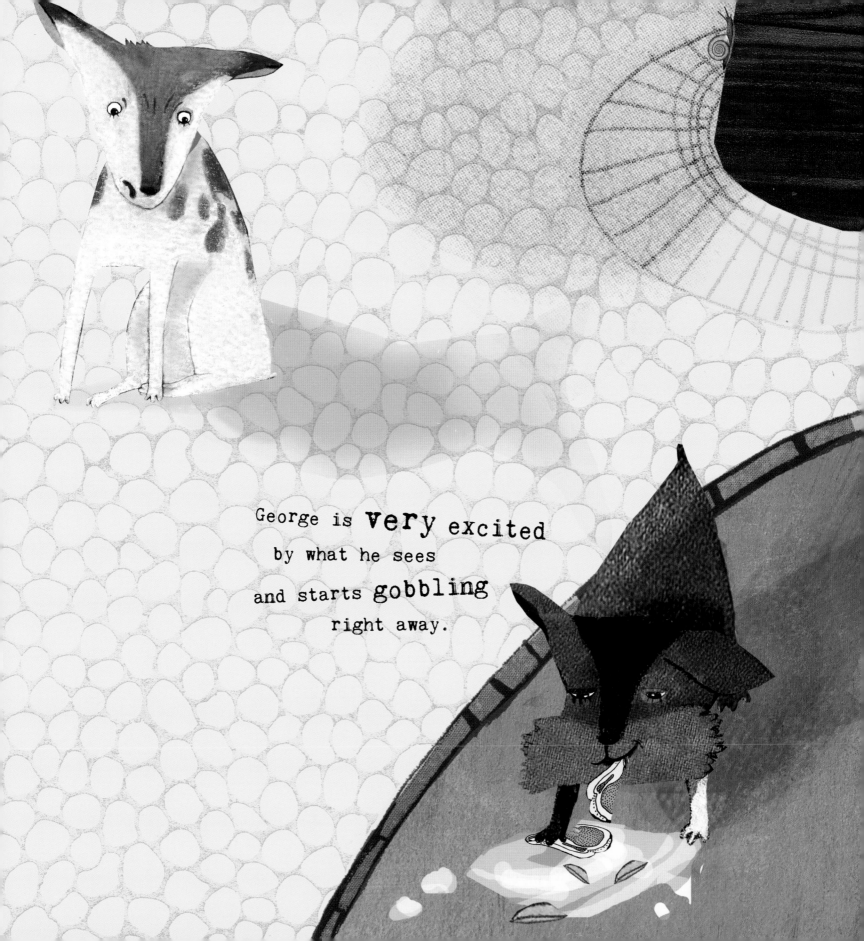

George is **very** excited
by what he sees
and starts **gobbling**
right away.

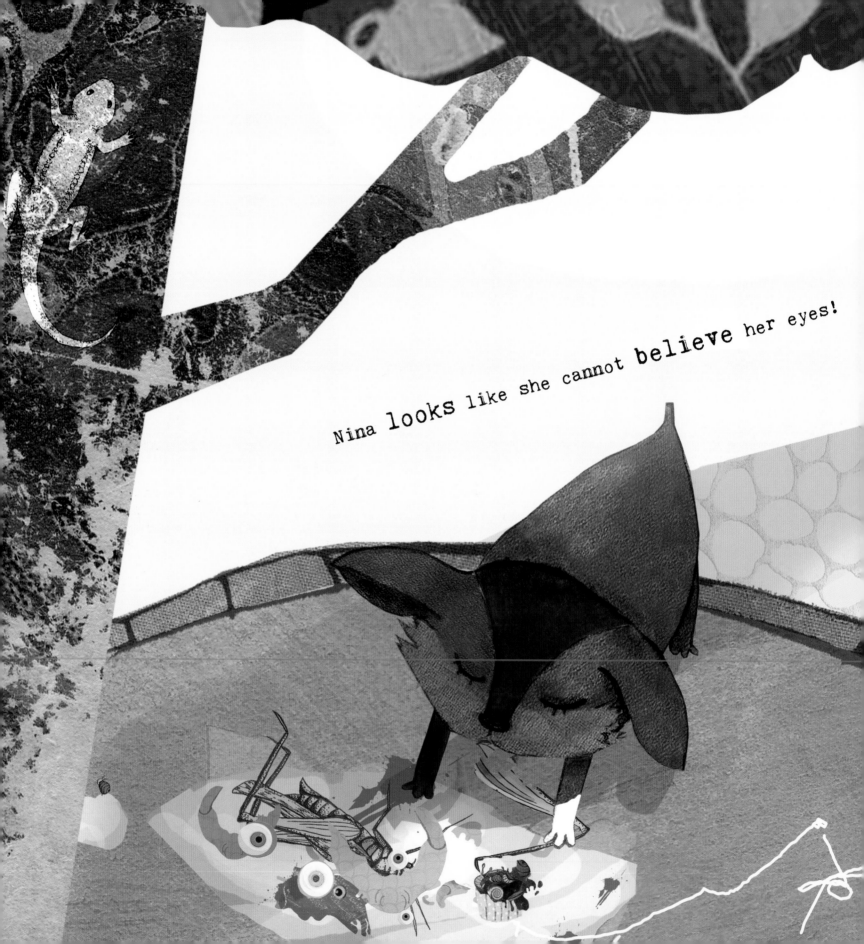

Nina looks like she cannot **believe** her eyes!

Nina stares at George
for a l o n g t i m e .

She looks at him like he's the **strangest** dog that ever lived on this earth.

I wonder what Nina would be saying
right **NOW** if she could talk...

The End

TV BRINGS THE
MOON LANDING TO EARTH

Rebecca Rissman

raintree
a Capstone company — publishers for children

Raintree is an imprint of Capstone Global Library Limited, a company incorporated in England and Wales having its registered office at 264 Banbury Road, Oxford, OX2 7DY – Registered company number: 6695582

www.raintree.co.uk
myorders@raintree.co.uk

Editor: Michelle Bisson
Designer: Tracy McCabe
Media Researcher: Svetlana Zhurkin
Production by Katy LaVigne
Printed and bound in India

ISBN 978 1 4747 6981 5

British Library Cataloguing in Publication Data
A full catalogue record for this book is available from the British Library.

Acknowledgements
We would like to thank the following for permission to reproduce photographs:
Getty Images: CBS Photo Archive, 31, 35, PhotoQuest, 11, ullstein bild/Quurke, 46; NASA, cover, 5, 6, 9, 14, 19, 20, 22, 25, 28, 29, 32, 37, 43, 44, 45, 48, 49, 51, 56 (top right and bottom), 57, 58, 59, Kim Shiflett, 54; Newscom: Universal Images Group/Sovfoto, 26, UPI/Jim Ruymen, 53, Zuma Press/Photoshot/Uppa, 12; Shutterstock: Aleks49, 17, 56 (top left).

We would like to thank Alan Schroeder, Professor, School of Journalism, Northeastern University, USA, for his invaluable help in the creation of this book.

Every effort has been made to contact copyright holders of material reproduced in this book. Any omissions will be rectified in subsequent printings if notice is given to the publisher.

All the internet addresses (URLs) given in this book were valid at the time of going to press. However, due to the dynamic nature of the internet, some addresses may have changed, or sites may have changed or ceased to exist since publication. While the author and publisher regret any inconvenience this may cause readers, no responsibility for any such changes can be accepted by either the author or the publisher.

CONTENTS

Chapter One

TENSION

At 4:18 pm on 20 July 1969, two astronauts felt the spidery legs of their spacecraft settle onto the surface of the Moon. The bleak, stark landing site was called the Sea of Tranquility. It was an ill-suited name for such a spot. It was desolate and dangerous, anything but tranquil – and not even a sea!

Astronaut Neil Armstrong spoke calmly into his headset radio: "Houston," he began. "Tranquility Base here. The *Eagle* has landed."

Around 394,300 kilometres (245,000 miles) away, NASA's Mission Control Center in Houston, Texas, USA, erupted into cheers. The giant room was filled with row after row of consoles. These were workstations for engineers, doctors, navigation specialists and technical advisers. Each person had a crucial role to play in keeping the astronauts alive, helping them land on the Moon, and then getting them back home to Earth safely.

The crew was radioed by the man sitting behind the Capsule Communication console (CAPCOM). "Roger, Tranquility. We copy you on the ground. You got a bunch of guys about to turn blue. We're breathing again. Thanks a lot."

NASA had just accomplished something amazing. It had sent a crew of astronauts on a mission called

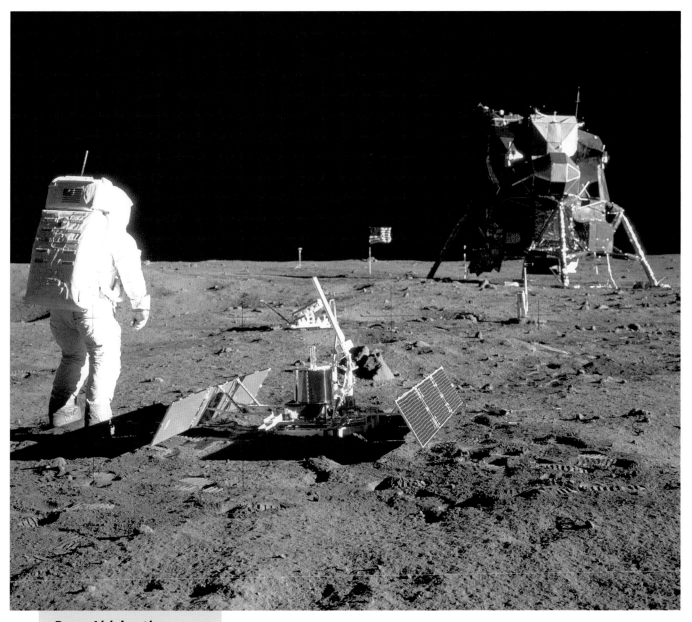

Buzz Aldrin, the second person to walk on the Moon, was photographed by Neil Armstrong, the first to do so.

Apollo 11 all the way to the Moon. Astronaut Michael Collins remained in a part of the spacecraft called the command module (CM). This orbited around the Moon. At the same time, two other astronauts, Neil Armstrong and Buzz Aldrin, rode a lunar module (LM) called *Eagle* down to the surface of the Moon.

No humans had ever landed on the Moon before. This was an amazing feat of engineering, science, bravery and creativity. But the crew of Apollo 11 hadn't finished yet. Aldrin and Armstrong were about to exit their spacecraft. Then they were going to attempt to walk on the Moon.

NASA planned to broadcast live television footage of the first-ever moonwalk. This would serve more than one purpose. Firstly, it would allow people across the globe to share in this historic achievement.

Secondly, it would prove that a Moon landing had, in fact, occurred. Many people at the time doubted that humans could travel to the Moon. Video footage would show them that it had really happened.

Armstrong and Aldrin were busy in the *Eagle*. They stepped into their bulky spacesuits and went over detailed checklists. They couldn't make any mistakes. As the astronauts got ready to step onto the powdery surface of the Moon, a young electrical engineer on Earth quietly panicked. His name was Stan Lebar. He was about to face the most stressful trial of his career. Lebar had created the video camera that would videotape the astronauts' moonwalk. This had been a very difficult task. The camera had to withstand the pressures of launch. It also had to be lightweight. It had to be durable enough to weather the very hot and very cold temperatures found in space.

Lebar didn't just create a video camera for this event. He also developed a special way to transmit the video footage from the Moon to Earth. It was a complex process. If everything went well, the astronauts' footage would follow a long, zigzagging course through space. The footage would bounce from the spacecraft's antenna to Earth, then up to satellites, before finally appearing on television screens around the world. It used brand-new technology. Lebar had tested and retested it, but he couldn't be sure it would work.

People around the world were excited about watching the first moonwalk. In the moments leading up to that event, more than half a billion viewers gathered around television sets. News stations had devoted hours of airtime to this story. Now everyone waited for the show of a lifetime.

Lebar nervously rubbed his lucky rabbit's foot. If the video footage didn't transmit from the Moon, NASA would say it was his fault. If something went wrong, Lebar would have to apologise to a global audience for his failure. His reputation and the hopes of millions of viewers were on the line.

NASA understood how important this mission was to the world. The agency made sure they captured every important moment on videotape. Cameras videotaped the action in Mission Control. One camera was mounted high in the room. Others were carried around by cameramen. This video was sent to news stations to broadcast to their viewers.

The minutes ticked by. Aldrin and Armstrong prepared to open the hatch of their spacecraft. This would expose them to the vacuum of space. The Moon has no oxygen to breathe. If their spacesuits weren't perfectly sealed, they would die.

Cameramen zoomed in on the stressed faces of the men in Mission Control and captured the tension in the room. Men studied stacks of papers. They double-checked their maths. Their instruments blinked. The room was hazy with cigarette smoke.

Mission Control was arranged a bit like a stadium. Four rows of consoles sat on ascending levels. The back row was the highest. This gave television viewers at home a glimpse of each of the consoles, blinking with electronics, and the men operating them. This set-up also gave everyone in Mission Control a clear view of the giant screens mounted on the front wall. In just a few moments, the screens might show the video footage transmitted from the surface of the Moon.

The astronauts' radio communication was piped into speakers mounted inside Mission Control. Armstrong's voice crackled over the radio. "The hatch is coming open." Men in Mission Control leaned forwards tensely at their consoles. They stared at the blank screen at the front of the room as they listened intently. Would the astronauts survive?

The hatch opened. Both astronauts continued speaking into their radios. They were fine.

Now it was time for the next step. Armstrong would climb out onto the "porch", or ladder, which was outside *Eagle*. Once there, he would tug on a little ring attached to a cord. This would open a small compartment and allow Lebar's camera to tumble into place. Inside *Eagle*, Aldrin would flip a switch to power up the camera.

Lebar's camera would point directly at the porch. This meant it would capture Armstrong's first movements on the Moon. If everything went according to plan, the large, blank screen in Mission Control was about to flicker to life with footage from the Moon.

Inside NASA's Manned Spacecraft Center, Lebar sweated. On the Moon, Armstrong spoke into his microphone: "I'm going to pull [the ring] now." The astronaut grasped the small metal ring and gave it a tug. Lebar's camera dropped perfectly into place.

CAPCOM spoke, "Roger, we copy. We're standing by for your TV."

In many places around the world, people huddled around television sets. No one knew exactly what they would see, or how it would look. As Lebar's camera hummed to life in space, each news channel switched

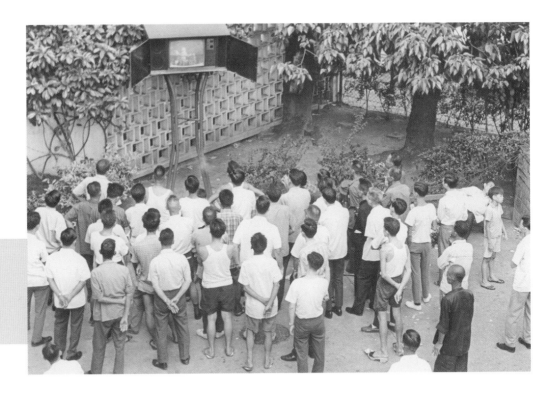

Worldwide, people came together to watch the Moon landing broadcast.

away from shots of its presenters or Mission Control. It was time to watch men walk on the Moon.

In Mission Control, a grey line flickered across the huge screen. Then a squiggle.

CAPCOM gasped: "Man, we're getting a picture on the TV."

Television screens across the globe glowed with the same footage. At first the images were hard to understand. They seemed to be upside down. Then the screen flickered and appeared to show the footage in negative. What should have been dark glowed bright white. Finally the picture resolved. A grainy black-and-white video showed an astronaut slowly climbing down a ladder.

Armstrong paused on the ladder's last step.

BROADCASTING TRAGEDY

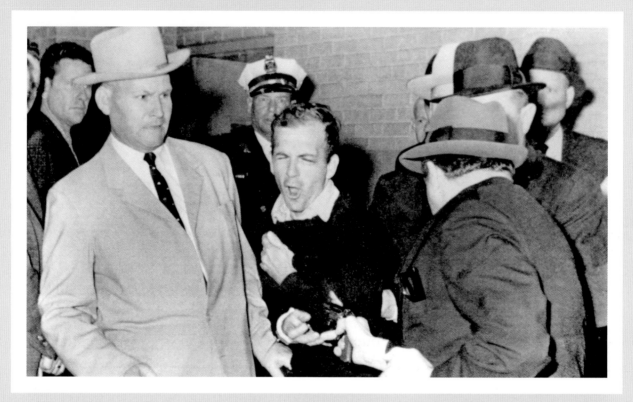

Viewers watched in real time as President Kennedy's alleged assassin was shot by a man named Jack Ruby.

In the 1960s, viewers had witnessed violent events on live television. In 1963 Lee Harvey Oswald assassinated US President John F. Kennedy. Later, news crews captured Oswald on live television as he walked to a county jail. While cameras rolled, Oswald was shot and killed by a nightclub owner named Jack Ruby. This was the first time someone had been murdered on live television in the United States.

Today many television stations insert a small delay between an event and the live television broadcast of it. This gives television producers time to interrupt the broadcast and prevent viewers from seeing something upsetting. NASA did not include a delay in the footage of its Moon landing. This meant that if something terrible occurred on the Moon, the world would see it happen live.

He was just centimetres from the surface of the Moon. The camera pointed directly at his feet. Armstrong described what he could see. The Moon's surface was covered in dust. "It's almost like a powder," he mused. "I'm going to step off the LM now." His voice sounded crackly because it was transmitted from so far away.

On-screen Armstrong seemed to take a big, slow-motion step down. His feet left the last rung of the ladder and sank slowly onto the surface of the Moon. Objects on the Moon have about one-sixth of the gravity they have on Earth. This means they are pulled towards the surface of the Moon with less force. Armstrong's descent from the ladder was the first live footage of someone moving in the reduced gravity of the Moon. It was an extraordinary sight.

The astronaut's boots settled into the fine Moon dust. Armstrong said, "That's one small step for man, one giant leap for mankind." As Armstrong took his first tentative steps on the Moon, newscasters on Earth did their best to narrate the scene. Many struggled to decipher the audio from the footage. On US channel NBC, Frank McGee couldn't understand Armstrong's declaration. Had he said, "One small step for man, one giant leap for man"? Static had interrupted the transmission in the middle of Armstrong's statement. Someone had to clarify the wording for him.

On CBS, newsreader Walter Cronkite was joined by Wally Schirra, an astronaut from earlier NASA missions. Schirra helped explain some of what the astronauts were experiencing. Cronkite's attention soon turned to the fact that the moonwalk was being broadcast.

"Boy, look at those pictures," he exclaimed.

Schirra couldn't get over his excitement at the footage. He said, "Oh, thank you, television for letting us watch this one." Cronkite commented, "Isn't this something? 240,000 miles out there on the Moon and we're seeing this history be made."

Armstrong continued exploring the Moon. He kicked up some dust and took a few more tentative hops. Soon, he helped Aldrin climb down onto the Moon as well.

About 600 million people watched the Moon landing. That was about one-sixth of the total global population at the time. Many children watched. At the time, not everyone owned a television set. This meant that many people had to watch it on a friend or neighbour's television or gather in public to watch. The broadcast of the moonwalk took place just after 10:30 pm Eastern Daylight Time (EDT) in America. In Europe, Asia and Australia it was very early in the morning, but millions tuned in. It was the first all-night broadcast on British television.

The Moon landing is believed to have had more viewers than any previous US television broadcast. The three national networks – ABC, NBC and CBS – all worked hard to ensure that their coverage would be perfect. They paid animators to create footage of spaceships travelling in space. They built mock lunar landers, then paid actors to wear spacesuits and pretend to pilot them. Adding such features to the broadcast helped viewers understand the complex space mission. They also helped to keep viewers interested and engaged. These elaborate productions were expensive. In all, the three news networks spent about $13 million on the broadcast.

As footage streamed through space of Armstrong and Aldrin walking on the Moon, one man on Earth sighed happily. Stan Lebar was delighted for NASA. He was also relieved. The camera worked! His camera worked.

Chapter Two

THE RACE TO THE MOON

On 4 October 1957, the Soviet Union launched the first human-made satellite into space. It was called *Sputnik. Sputnik* collected information about Earth's atmosphere. It also recorded the temperature inside the satellite and on its outer surface. *Sputnik* sent this information down to Earth with a beeping signal. By today's standards *Sputnik* was very simple. In 1957, however, it represented a huge advance in technology.

The United States and the Soviet Union had been allies in World War II, but their political systems were at odds. In the late 1940s, Soviet leaders aggressively expanded their country's communist influence in Eastern Europe. Soviet armed forces, called the Red Army, occupied many countries, including Poland, Hungary and Bulgaria. The Union of Soviet Socialist Republics (USSR) worked to convert its new territories to communism. Soviet leaders sometimes used violence to accomplish this goal.

For their part, Americans were distrustful of the Soviet Union. They believed communism was wrong. Instead, they thought that capitalism was a better and more sustainable economic and political system. Americans did not like to see communism growing in Eastern Europe.

The relationship between the Soviet Union and

A model of the first *Sputnik* can be viewed in a museum in Moscow, Russia.

the US grew more strained over the years. Each side wanted to show that it was superior. The two world powers worked to develop their armed forces and technologies. If war ever broke out between them, each side wanted to be prepared to win. This state of tension was called the Cold War (1945–1991).

When the Soviets launched *Sputnik*, they expanded the Cold War with a battle known as the space race. This was the contest between the US and the Soviet Union to show dominance in space exploration. Each side wanted to make advances in space first. At the time many people wondered if humans could live on the Moon or other planets. People thought countries might be able to expand into territories out in space. They also feared that weapons would be launched from space. The US and the USSR both wanted to get to space first. This would help them show their power and control.

After *Sputnik* the Soviets continued to enjoy a lead in the space race. On 3 November 1957, the Soviets sent the first animal into space. It was a dog named Laika. On 12 April 1961, a Soviet cosmonaut named Yuri Gagarin became the first human to fly into space in a space capsule called the *Vostok-1*. He flew for 108 minutes and orbited Earth once.

The United States followed with its own small achievements in space. In 1958 President Dwight D. Eisenhower authorised the creation of an American space agency. It was called the National Aeronautics and Space Administration (NASA). NASA hired people to launch satellites. At NASA people also worked on new, powerful rockets. NASA hoped to send a human up into space quickly.

John F. Kennedy became president in 1961. He believed that the US should prioritise space exploration. He thought that a strong space

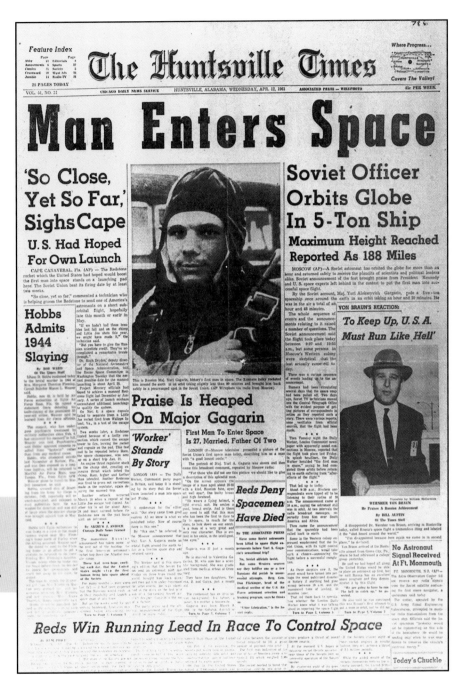

Yuri Gagarin's trip into space was front-page news in the US.

programme would boost American spirits. Kennedy and his vice president, Lyndon B. Johnson, were both very excited about stepping up the space race. They encouraged people at NASA to work hard to beat the Soviets.

President Kennedy
was considered
very bold when he
announced the goal of
landing a man on the
Moon before the end
of the 1960s.

NASA sent Alan Shepard into space on board
a space capsule called *Freedom 7* on 5 May 1961.
Shepard's mission was a success. However, it was
very short. It lasted just 15 minutes. This was less
than one-seventh of the time Soviet cosmonaut
Gagarin had flown in space. Shepard did not orbit
Earth. He flew in a simple, short arc. The US was
losing the space race.

Twenty days after Shepard's mission, Kennedy
made a speech to Congress. He said, "I believe that
this nation should commit itself to achieving the
goal, before this decade is out, of landing a man on

"I believe that this nation should commit itself to achieving the goal . . . of landing a man on the Moon."

the Moon and returning him safely to the Earth." This was an ambitious goal. NASA did not yet have the technology, experience, expertise, scientific knowledge, training or money that would be needed to send a man to the Moon.

But NASA soon began developing a plan to accomplish Kennedy's goal. The agency would work towards a Moon mission in stages. The first stage, already under way, was called Project Mercury. This was a set of missions using a simple spaceship, or capsule, called *Mercury*. Shepard had travelled in a *Mercury* capsule into space.

On 20 February 1962, John Glenn orbited Earth three times in a *Mercury* capsule. His mission showed that NASA was starting to catch up to the Soviets in the space race. Television news covered Glenn's mission breathlessly. News producers switched from coverage of newsreaders at their desks to long-distance camera shots of Glenn's rocket on its launchpad. When the countdown reached zero and the rocket lurched into the air, CBS newsreader Walter Cronkite couldn't contain his excitement. He yelped, "Go, baby!" The three national US networks all aired the launch. More than 40 million people watched.

After Project Mercury, NASA moved on to Project Gemini. These were more complex, two-passenger spacecraft. Gemini spacecraft were able to dock,

or pair up, with another spacecraft while in space.
Some Gemini astronauts could exit their capsules and
float freely in space – known as a spacewalk. Project
Gemini helped NASA develop the skills necessary
for a Moon mission, which would probably require
astronauts to steer, dock and exit their spaceship.

As the US manned space programme advanced,
television also evolved. In the 1960s the three major
networks expanded their nightly news programmes
from 15 to 30 minutes. These broadcasts kept viewers
informed of current events.

Television news channels also cut into other
programmes during times of crisis. On 22 November

1963, daytime television viewers were startled to see their programmes interrupted. Journalists appeared on each of the networks with a troubling announcement. President Kennedy had been shot. Viewers watched, rapt, as the story developed. They eventually learned that the president had been killed. Vice President Johnson would assume the presidency. Allowing the news to break into other programming showed that the news was urgent and important.

In the 1960s, the topics covered by television news broadcasts were often very controversial. The Vietnam War, for example, was an event that was widely covered on television, and that divided the nation. Video footage showed graphic glimpses of the battlegrounds in Vietnam, and then covered anti-war protests in the US. Many did not agree about what to do in Vietnam. Some wanted the United States to leave the conflict, while others wanted it to stay and fight. The nightly news highlighted this divide.

Television news producers thought that the US space programme could unite the country. Networks dedicated themselves to covering NASA's space missions. These exciting spectacles were a welcome relief from controversial news. News segments focusing on NASA's early space missions gave Americans the chance to unite in support of the nation's astronauts and in their desire to win the space race by beating the Soviets to the Moon.

Television news crews worked hard to create dynamic coverage of NASA's missions. They invited expert guests to appear on camera. They also often extended their air time. Astronauts sometimes sat next to newsreaders on camera. They helped explain the science and excitement of these missions to the public.

But before NASA accomplished its first spacewalk, the Soviets swooped in with another victory. On 18 March 1965, Soviet cosmonaut Alexei Leonov exited his spacecraft while orbiting Earth. He performed a 12-minute spacewalk. The Soviets televised this event. Soviet viewers watched with delight as Leonov floated in space.

Three months later, astronaut Ed White performed the first US spacewalk from a Gemini capsule. His 23-minute spacewalk was broadcast on television. As White floated in space, he exclaimed, "I feel like a million dollars!"

After Gemini, NASA moved forwards with its next phase, Project Apollo. Engineers hoped that Apollo would bring NASA's astronauts to the Moon. Landing a spaceship on the Moon was incredibly complicated. But what made it even more difficult was that NASA also wanted to get the spaceship home. This meant they had to design a spacecraft to fly to the Moon, land, and take off again.

NASA came up with a complicated plan for

"I feel like a million dollars!"

In 1965 astronaut Ed White made history with the first US spacewalk.

Project Apollo. It was called Lunar Orbit Rendezvous (LOR). This involved sending a three-part spacecraft into space. One part was the command module (CM). This held a cockpit big enough for three astronauts. Another component was called the service module. This held the main power supply and oxygen the astronauts needed. The last component was called the lunar module (LM). This was a small spacecraft with its own engines. Two astronauts could climb

SOVIET SECRETS

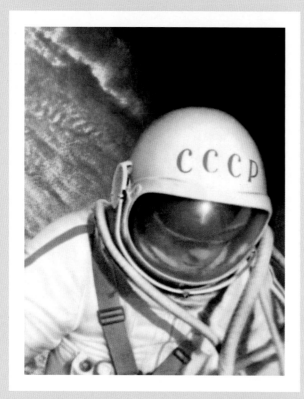

Alexei Leonov made history with his spacewalk. The unknown story is that he almost died doing so.

Few people knew that Alexei Leonov nearly died at the end of his spacewalk. His spacesuit had become overfilled with oxygen. He struggled to move his arms and legs. His hands slipped out of his gloves. His boots stretched away from his feet. Leonov needed to climb back into his spacecraft. This was impossible in his balloon-like suit. Leonov did something dangerous and drastic. He opened a valve in his suit. This released oxygen out into space. It partially deflated his suit, but it could have killed him. If too much oxygen drained out, he would have died from a lack of the vital gas. But Leonov was lucky. He climbed back into his spacecraft alive.

This information was not released until after the fall of the Soviet Union. Before that the Soviets tried hard to show a perfect image of their space programme. They did not want anyone to know about their problems.

into it and separate from the rest of their craft. The LM's small engines were powerful enough to move it through space. When they were ready, the astronauts in the LM could reconnect, or dock, with the rest of their spacecraft.

LOR was NASA's best shot at a Moon landing. But it was still very risky. It required the team of three astronauts to split up. One would remain in the CM. He would orbit the Moon. The other two would fly down to the surface of the Moon in the LM. When they were ready, they would use a small engine on the LM to launch themselves back up into space. Then the CM and LM would have to meet up perfectly in space to dock. After that all three astronauts would sit in the CM cockpit. They would fire a series of powerful engines. These would send them back to Earth.

Project Apollo utilised many brand-new technologies. Much of what NASA was attempting to do was not yet understood. No one knew exactly what awaited the astronauts on the Moon. Some people thought that they might find aliens there. Others worried that the Moon would be toxic. They feared that the astronauts would die.

Though President Kennedy had died, the space programme still worked to meet his goal of landing a man on the Moon by 1970. President Johnson led the charge, urging NASA to work quickly and lobbying Congress to provide the necessary funding. Despite Johnson's support, NASA could not build everything it needed on its own. So, NASA hired a company to build the command and service modules for the Apollo mission. Some of the astronauts worried that the first Apollo capsules hadn't been constructed well.

Astronaut Gus Grissom was scheduled to fly on the first Apollo mission. This mission would test out the Apollo spacecraft. Grissom said the spacecraft was a lemon. This meant that he thought it was unsafe. NASA engineers worked hard to fix all of its problems,

(Left to right): Apollo 1 astronauts Gus Grissom, Ed White, and Roger Chaffee. They died during a practice launch.

but Grissom was pessimistic. The day he left for the launch rehearsal, Grissom picked a lemon from a tree in his garden. His wife asked him why he'd done it and Grissom responded, "I'm going to hang it on that spacecraft." Grissom never returned home.

On 27 January 1967, Grissom and two other crew members, Ed White and Roger Chaffee, climbed into their Apollo command module. They were practising for an upcoming launch. A wire sparked inside their spacecraft and a fire started. Inside the command module, the astronauts breathed 100 per cent oxygen.

The intense heat of the fire that killed the Apollo 1 astronauts can even be seen on the outside of the damaged command module.

This is a very flammable gas. Many things inside the command module were made from flammable materials. An explosive fire erupted. The astronauts were trapped. All three men died within moments. This tragedy reminded Americans that spaceflight was still very dangerous.

But the danger of spaceflight wasn't the only obstacle NASA had to overcome in its mission to get humans to the Moon. There was also a growing public reluctance to fund the expensive agency. In 1961, when Kennedy challenged NASA to land a man on the Moon, many Americans were excited by the idea. However, as years passed, some people grew weary of the expensive space agency. NASA was paid for out of the national budget. In total, the Apollo programme would cost the US government more than $25 billion. People at NASA wanted to show Americans that the work and money they had put into the space programme was worth it. They knew that a television broadcast of the Moon landing would help to show everyone what their money had paid for.

Televising the Moon landing also required new technology. Ordinary film cameras weighed as much as 300 kilograms (700 pounds) and used a lot of power to run. NASA needed small, lightweight, energy-efficient cameras to take into space. Stan Lebar worked for five years to create the right camera for space missions. A team of 75 engineers helped. The camera was very impressive. It weighed 3.17 kg (7 pounds) and used just 7 watts of electricity. The camera was also durable. It could survive the extreme temperatures of space. That meant it would still work between minus 160 and 185 degrees Celsius (minus 250 and 300 degrees Fahrenheit).

It could also capture images in the bright sun and dark shadows of the Moon. Lebar gave NASA the perfect tool to capture the Moon landing. Now NASA just had to get its astronauts to the Moon.

Project Apollo proceeded quickly. NASA launched the first crewed mission, Apollo 7, in October 1968. And then, in December 1968, Apollo 8 orbited the Moon.

Richard M. Nixon was inaugurated as president in January 1969. He was eager to see the US succeed in the space race. He watched excitedly as Apollo 9 launched in March, and Apollo 10 followed

CBS news presenter Walter Cronkite taped a programme on Apollo 8 at the Hayden Planetarium in New York.

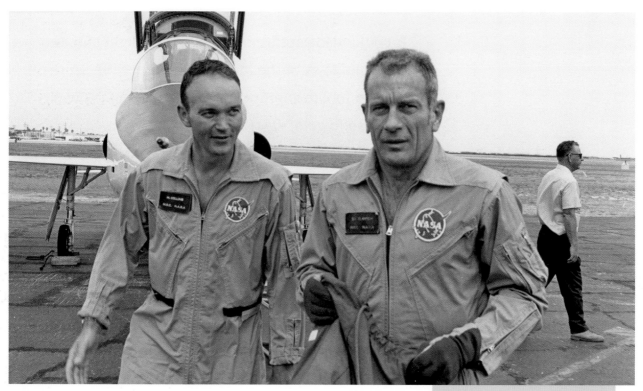

Michael Collins (left) and Deke Slayton arrived together for the Apollo 11 launch.

in May. These missions helped astronauts to practise the skills they needed for a Moon landing. By the summer of 1969, NASA was ready to try to land the crew of Apollo 11 on the Moon.

Deke Slayton, Chief of the Astronaut Office, chose the crew. Slayton had a motto: "Any crew can fly any mission". This meant that any NASA astronaut with the right training and background could succeed in any mission to which he was assigned.

For Apollo 11 Slayton chose Michael Collins, an experienced Air Force pilot and Gemini astronaut, to be the command module pilot. This role required excellent flight skills and attention to detail. For the lunar module pilot, Slayton chose Buzz Aldrin.

Aldrin was an Air Force pilot and Gemini astronaut with a PhD in aeronautics and astronautics. Slayton named Neil Armstrong as the mission's commander. Armstrong, now a civilian, was a former naval aviator and test pilot. He had a degree in engineering and had commanded Gemini 8.

Armstrong, Aldrin and Collins trained for seven months. Though Armstrong and Aldrin would walk on the Moon, Collins was not disappointed by his assignment. He knew that his role flying the command module around the Moon by himself was crucial. He also looked forward to achieving a space first of his own. He would become the first human to orbit the Moon by himself.

As the launch date for Apollo 11 approached, people at NASA argued about who would be the first man to walk on the Moon. Aldrin thought it should be him. In Gemini flights, the pilot, not the commander, left the spacecraft. But Slayton thought that the senior astronaut should get the honour. Armstrong had been at NASA for one year longer than Aldrin. Also, the LM's door to the outside was on Armstrong's side. The astronauts' bulky spacesuits meant it would be hard for Aldrin to climb over Armstrong to make his exit. In the end, NASA decided: Armstrong would be first.

Now all NASA had to do was get its crew to the Moon. And bring them home again.

Chapter Three

THE MISSION

On 16 July 1969, news presenter Walter Cronkite sat behind his CBS news desk. A countdown to the launch of Apollo 11 played across the bottom of the screen. Cronkite told his viewers all about the upcoming mission. Apollo 11 would launch using powerful rockets. Then it would loop around Earth once. After that it would fire a rocket to thrust it towards the Moon.

When the countdown reached zero, Apollo 11's rockets blasted it off the launchpad. Cronkite could hardly contain himself. "Oh boy. Oh, boy, it looks good," he exclaimed. The spacecraft zoomed up into the sky. It travelled faster and faster. The television camera crews struggled to keep it in their frames.

In addition to Cronkite and his guest commentator, astronaut Wally Schirra, several voices from inside Mission Control at NASA were audible to the television audience. NASA allowed news stations to access some of its radio communications. This helped Americans feel connected to their space programme.

This decision to allow the public to hear its communications was unusual. Before this, many US agencies were very private. Emergencies were sometimes reported only after they had occurred. Even then, many agencies released little information

Astronaut Wally Schirra (left) and news presenter Walter Cronkite talked on the field before the launch of Apollo 11.

to the public. NASA was different. It allowed journalists to sit in a special section of Mission Control. They were allowed to watch events from this important room as they happened. NASA also released the record of its communication with its space crews after the flights. This was partly in response to the secretive Soviet space programme. The Soviets often kept their space missions a secret until after they were complete. By being open with the public, NASA stood out as different.

Meanwhile, as Apollo 11 began its long journey to the Moon, most normal television programming resumed. Viewers were updated on Apollo 11's progress every night on the news shows.

The astronauts sent short television broadcasts down to Earth. News stations picked up these videos and played them for their audiences. The videos let viewers know what the astronauts were doing. They also provided an interesting glimpse into life in space. On 17 July, Michael Collins showed television viewers the astronauts' neatly packaged, freeze-dried food. On 18 July, Armstrong and Aldrin sent a short video as they floated around in their spacesuits. As the Moon landing grew nearer, news networks devoted more and more time to the upcoming event.

On 19 July, Apollo 11 was coming close to the Moon. A set of rockets on the spacecraft fired. These knocked it into orbit around the Moon. The astronauts had been in space for almost 76 hours. It was almost time for them to attempt the first-ever Moon landing.

On Sunday 20 July 1969, CBS began its marathon coverage. CBS planned to devote 31 hours straight to the event, boasting that the Moon landing would be "a most historic event, but our own coverage will be up to matching it." Newsreaders on all three networks informed their viewers of exactly what was happening in space. They told them that the crew on board Apollo 11 was looping around the Moon. They were almost 394,300 km (245,000 miles) from Earth.

At about noon, Houston time, the crew of Apollo 11 was ready to reach the Moon. It was time to separate the different parts of the spacecraft.

Eagle – the lunar module – was photographed in space from the command module, **Columbia.**

Astronauts Neil Armstrong and Buzz Aldrin climbed into *Eagle*. Collins stayed in the command module, *Columbia*. He would keep orbiting the Moon while Aldrin and Armstrong travelled down to the Moon's surface. At 12:18 pm, Armstrong and Aldrin were buckled into the cockpit of *Eagle*. Collins pushed a button in his cockpit. This sent *Eagle* floating out into space. As the LM drifted away. Collins told the two, "Okay, there you go! Beautiful!" Armstrong used a set of controls on his side of the LM cockpit to steady *Eagle*.

The two spacecraft looped around the Moon once together. Collins double-checked that his command module was working perfectly. He needed to be sure he would be able to meet up with *Eagle* after the Moon landing. Aldrin and Armstrong were busy in *Eagle*. They worked quickly to prepare for their trip to the Moon's surface.

Soon, *Eagle*'s engines fired. These sent Aldrin and Armstrong down towards the Moon. Much of *Eagle*'s flight was controlled by computer. This device used radar to sense where to send the spacecraft.

Television viewers who tuned in to CBS watched an animated version of *Eagle* descending through space. Orange flames shot from its engines. Just below it was a large clock counting down until the anticipated time of the Moon landing. The voices of the astronauts, Mission Control, Cronkite and Schirra all narrated the scene. Occasionally a set of numbers flashed over the animation. These described *Eagle*'s speed, height and distance to the Moon to give viewers the feeling that they were fully informed about the mission. Of course, television viewers could really see only pre-recorded animated images. The images did not match the exact progress of *Eagle*'s actual descent, which they could not see.

In fact, as Schirra and Cronkite spoke calmly to their television viewers about the astronauts' mission, Aldrin and Armstrong experienced an emergency on

"What's this alarm, Wally?"

board *Eagle*. It is clearly audible on the news broadcast. But as Schirra and Cronkite didn't know what was happening, they did not inform their viewers. Therefore, few people understood exactly what was going on.

While Aldrin and Armstrong approached the Moon, an alarm rang out inside *Eagle*. Aldrin had never heard this type of alarm before. He wondered what it meant. Armstrong's voice snapped over the radio: "Programme alarm!" Cronkite and Schirra continued to narrate the footage casually and confidently. They joked a little and reminded their viewers that the Moon landing was minutes away.

On the ground, people in Mission Control scrambled to understand *Eagle*'s alarm. A computer expert in Mission Control thought that the LM's computer was overloaded. It could not handle all the information it was processing. The alarm simply alerted the crew of this. He thought the men should still try to land on the Moon. Mission Control told the astronauts: "We're go on that alarm." In other words, they could continue their mission.

The alarm rang out again. This time Cronkite paid attention. "What's this alarm, Wally?" Schirra explained that it had to do with the computers on board *Eagle*, but that the crew was still "Go". His voice sounded calm.

News networks occasionally switched away from their presenters or the animated *Eagle*. They showed crowds at airports, at Disneyland or on the street watching the footage of the Moon landing. This contributed to the feeling that the whole world was watching.

Eagle dropped down towards the surface of the Moon. At 3,000 feet (914 metres) CAPCOM told the crew: "You're GO for landing." As Eagle descended, more alarms rang out inside the ship. The lunar module's computer was still having trouble handling all of the information it was processing. The astronauts reported these alarms to Mission Control, but again, Cronkite and Schirra ignored them. They focused instead on their excitement at the upcoming Moon landing. Mission Control told the crew they were still clear to land.

Armstrong expertly steered Eagle towards a flat, safe landing place. News channels continued to play the astronauts' communications to Mission Control. These were technical readings from their instruments. They meant little to the average viewer. To keep things exciting, the stations switched to animated Moons and actors wearing spacesuits pretending to fly spacecraft.

But news presenters and their guests fell silent as the astronauts closed in on the Moon. It seemed as though they didn't want to interrupt this historic moment with their own narration. They simply let their viewers listen to the technical communications between the astronauts and Mission Control.

"You're GO for landing."

"You guys
are getting
prime TV
time!"

It took longer than expected for Armstrong to land *Eagle*. This meant that ABC's animation showed a Moon lander touching down minutes before the actual *Eagle* made contact with the Moon's surface. While Armstrong and Aldrin coasted over its surface, ABC viewers watched footage of actors dressed as astronauts inside a mock cockpit. Then the screen switched back to the animated lander resting on the surface of the Moon. When Armstrong finally lowered *Eagle* expertly onto the surface of the Moon at 4:17 pm EDT, ABC showed the animated LM touching down once again.

Shortly after bringing *Eagle* down onto the Moon, Armstrong shut down his engines and looked at Aldrin. The two men smiled at each other. They had done it! They clasped bulky, gloved hands for a moment.

Armstrong and Aldrin had planned to wait on the surface of the Moon for several hours before leaving *Eagle*. But both men were ready to explore. They radioed Mission Control to ask if they could take their moonwalk five hours earlier than planned. CAPCOM responded immediately that they could: "You guys are getting prime television time!"

Armstrong and Aldrin put their spacesuits on. They snapped their airtight helmets and gloves onto their thick suits. These would protect them from the harsh environment on the Moon. Finally, at 9:28 pm

EDT, they opened *Eagle*'s door. Outside, they saw the grey, rocky surface of the Moon. Armstrong pulled on the cord that let a video camera fall into place on the outside of *Eagle*. Aldrin switched it on.

The camera started rolling. It transmitted an electronic signal to tracking stations in Australia and California. In Australia the signal was converted into video. This video signal then went back up into space to satellites. The satellites bounced the video down to Mission Control in Houston. Finally, from there, the video went out to news networks. This was a long and complex path for the signal. This, along with the smaller bandwidth size, reduced the quality of the video. Though the original footage was crisp, the images that made it to televisions on Earth were grainy and looked blurry.

Armstrong took his first shaky steps on the Moon at 9:39 pm EDT. Then Aldrin joined him. The men collected rock samples. They hopped around and joked a little. Armstrong set up a tripod about 12 metres (40 feet) from *Eagle*. He then took the camera from the outside of *Eagle* and put it on top of the tripod. This expanded the view for their television audiences. Instead of just pointing at the side of their LM, it now showed a wide view of the Moon.

News presenterss remained mostly silent during the moonwalk. They let television viewers listen to the astronauts and the crews in Mission Control.

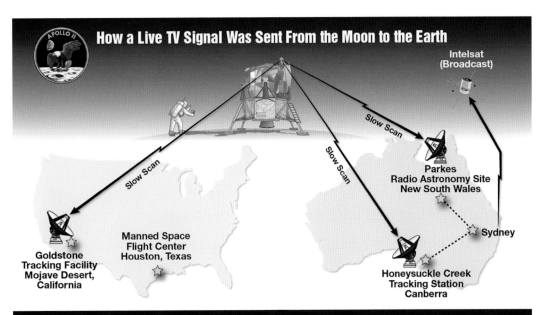

How a Live TV Signal Was Sent From the Moon to the Earth

How a Live TV Signal Was Sent From the Moon to the Earth

TV signals were sent from the Moon to different places on Earth.

Occasionally text would flash across the video with messages such as "LIVE FROM THE SURFACE OF THE MOON". This helped viewers who had just tuned in know exactly what they were seeing.

Aldrin and Armstrong planted a US flag on the Moon. Because there is no wind on the Moon, the flagpole included a horizontal bar to keep the flag unfurled. The two men stood back to look at it. Just then a voice crackled into their headset radios. It was President Richard Nixon. He wanted to talk to them.

Television screens on Earth showed Nixon sitting at his desk. Occasionally the image split to show both the president and the astronauts on the Moon. Holding a phone to one ear, Nixon told them that their moonwalk was uniting everyone on the planet. "For one priceless moment, in the whole history of man, all the people on this earth are truly one. One in their pride in what you have done." Armstrong thanked the president. He said, "It's a great honour and privilege for us to be here, representing not only the United States but men of peace of all nations . . . men with a vision for the future."

Aldrin and Armstrong planted the US flag on the Moon – winning that part of the space race.

THE LOST MOON LANDING VIDEOTAPES

NASA Archive   2009 Restoration

These stills show the Moon landing footage before and after the restoration of the videotapes.

During the Moon landing, NASA recorded the raw video footage sent from *Apollo 11*. This footage had not yet been converted to the smaller bandwidth. This meant that it was much clearer than what television viewers saw. The images were crisper and easier to understand.

In 2004 historians began to look for this original footage. It had been recorded on tapes of magnetic film. The historians could not find it. In 2006 NASA acknowledged that the footage was probably gone.

To save money back in the 1970s and 1980s NASA reused its magnetic tapes. The agency believed it was likely that the Moon landing video had been erased so that the tapes could be reused for another purpose.

Video technicians have worked to restore the footage that was broadcast back in 1969. They carefully removed static and made the images as crisp as possible. These restored videos offer a better view of what the first Moon landing was really like.

Finally, after two and a half hours, the astronauts returned to *Eagle*. They rested inside the small cockpit and prepared to reunite with the command module. At 12:54 pm EDT on Monday 21 July 1969, a

President Nixon talked to the astronauts while they were on the Moon.

set of rockets fired underneath *Eagle*. These launched it off the surface of the Moon. *Eagle* soon started orbiting the Moon. Four hours later Collins watched as *Eagle* approached his command module. Armstrong expertly flew *Eagle*. The spacecraft docked perfectly. Collins was glad to see his friends again.

Soon the three astronauts gathered in the command module. *Eagle* was not built to withstand the journey back through Earth's atmosphere. The astronauts did not need it anymore. Collins flipped a switch to separate the command module from the LM. Then, *Eagle* went out into space.

On Thursday 22 July, the astronauts fired their engines again. This time the thrust sent them back towards Earth. The three astronauts safely splashed down into the Pacific Ocean on Thursday 24 July 1969.

ChapterFour
A LASTING IMPACT

The Apollo 11 mission lasted eight days. Neil Armstrong and Buzz Aldrin's moonwalk took just two and a half hours. But thanks in no small part to the extensive television coverage of this event, its significance has endured.

NASA has estimated that more than one half of the entire global population was aware of the Moon landing. In addition to the 600 million people who watched it on live television, others listened to it on the radio. Even more saw footage of it later. Many read about it in newspapers or magazines.

America's Cold War enemy, the Soviet Union, tried to block broadcasts of the Moon landing. But many Soviet citizens still found out about it. Some people thought that, with the US landing on the Moon, the space race was over. Others disagreed. The Soviets didn't give up. They sent un-crewed lunar landers to the Moon. But their programme was very expensive and plagued by faulty rockets and equipment. Eventually the Soviets abandoned their goal of landing a human on the Moon. Instead, the Soviet space agency shifted focus. It focused on other space missions, such as Earth-orbiting space stations.

President Nixon greeted the astronauts after they returned to Earth. He told them, "This is the greatest

New York City welcomed home the Apollo 11 crew with a ticker-tape parade.

week in the history of the world since creation." A big part of what made the Moon mission so important was that NASA shared it with the world. People living across the globe were able to watch the event as it happened. Many people believed that this experience connected them.

The Moon landing united people who were excited about space travel. One French scholar remarked on the mission's incredible impact: "Americans reached out and touched the Moon. But it was a victory for the indomitable spirit of every man."

Apollo 17 astronaut Gene Cernan test-drove the lunar rover on the Moon.

In the years after Apollo 11, NASA sent five additional crews to the Moon. Astronauts on these missions walked on the Moon. Some drove a simple car called a rover across the lunar surface. They did science experiments. Over time, the public's excitement about space travel faded. Fewer viewers tuned in to watch the missions' televised broadcasts. Project Apollo ended in 1972. In 1975 the US and Soviets launched a co-operative space mission called Apollo-Soyuz. Three American astronauts met up with two Soviet cosmonauts in space. They docked their spacecraft together and shook hands. This joint mission marked the unofficial end of the space race.

Though the initial excitement over the Moon landing faded, its video footage remains important. The Moon landing video has been reused and repurposed many times. Filmmakers have included clips from the Moon landing in documentaries about space travel. Artists have used the footage for video art installations. Other artists have painted still images from the video footage. Famous pop artist Andy Warhol created a series of silkscreens in 1987 called *Moonwalk*. They show Buzz Aldrin standing next to the US flag. Warhol painted each in different vibrant colours. In 2016 a set of two *Moonwalk* prints sold in London for £185,000.

Some artists evoke the importance of the Moon landing without using any of the visual images at all. Artist On Kawara creates large black-and-white paintings that show important dates. In Kawara's Today series, three paintings are hung next to one another. They read *July 16, 1969*; *July 20, 1969* and *July 21, 1969*. Beneath and beside the paintings are boxes filled with newspapers. Headlines declaring "Man Walks on Moon" explain the dates to viewers. Kawara's art assumes that the Moon landing is important enough that just seeing the dates will evoke emotions in those who look at the paintings.

The Moon landing also inspired books and poetry. Writers had mixed opinions about sending humans to the Moon. Some were thrilled. Others were wary.

WAS THE MOON LANDING A HOAX?

The US flag is propped up with a clearly visible horizontal bar.

In the 1960s, the idea that humans could land on the Moon was hard for many people to understand. Some doubted that it was possible. After Apollo 11 made it to the Moon, a small number of people believed that the mission had been faked. They thought that NASA had worked with a film studio to create the footage broadcast on television news.

In 1969 the idea that the Moon landing was fake, or a hoax, was unpopular. Polls showed that fewer than 5 per cent of people "doubted the Moon voyage had taken place". Over time, however, that number has grown. A 2004 poll showed that 27 per cent of Americans between the ages of 18 and 24 "expressed doubts that NASA went to the Moon".

People who do not believe that Apollo 11 made it to the Moon make several arguments. They note that the US flag planted on the Moon should not appear to fly, as it does on film, because the Moon has no wind.

This is true. But the flag does not fly. It is propped up with a horizontal bar. Others have suggested that the shadows visible on the Moon do not look natural. They believe they were created by stage lighting in a film studio. NASA has explained that these shadows were created by the special camera lenses and sloping terrain of the Moon.

Several Apollo astronauts have struggled to accept that people doubt their accomplishments. Harrison Schmitt, Apollo 17 astronaut, has said, "If people decide they're going to deny the facts of history and the facts of science and technology, there's not much you can do with them. For most of them, I just feel sorry that we failed in their education." In 2002 Buzz Aldrin was confronted by a man who thought he had faked his moonwalk. The man called Aldrin "a coward, a liar, and a thief". Aldrin, then 72, punched the man in the face.

British poet W. H. Auden was thankful that the astronauts did not spoil the Moon. One month after the Apollo 11 mission, he penned a poem called "Moon Landing" with the words "Unsmudged, thank God, my Moon still queens the Heavens."

The video footage of the Moon landing has had a lasting impact on popular culture. One of the most obvious examples of this comes from the MTV network. The creators of MTV wanted unique animation for their new music network. They hired a graphic design firm to create the animation, headed by a designer named Pat Gorman. Gorman and her team used footage from the Moon landing in the animation. It showed the astronauts planting the US flag on the Moon. Instead of the stars and stripes, they modified the video footage to show flashing, multicoloured patterns on the flag. Gorman said, "We thought, 'We're like the guys landing on the Moon and claiming it. We claim this land for music.'"

MTV aired its first broadcast in 1981. It opened with the famous Moon landing animation. MTV played this animation at the beginning of every hour of programming for its first five years. This exposed a new generation of viewers to this famous video.

Footage from the Moon landing has made its way into many different elements of pop culture. A 1992 episode of *The Simpsons* used the audio from the Moon landing in a flashback. In it, Homer Simpson's

"We're like the guys landing on the Moon and claiming it. We claim this land for music."

Kendrick Lamar won six MTV awards in 2017. The trophies each show an astronaut holding the flag, a tribute to Apollo 11.

dad watches the news footage while Homer sits nearby, ignoring the event.

Other shows have not used the exact footage but have recalled the story of the broadcast itself. *Futurama* and *Doctor Who* have both featured the Moon landing broadcast in episodes. Films have also relied on the story of the Apollo 11 mission. *Transformers: Dark of the Moon, Men in Black 3* and many other films have recalled this mission. In 2018 a movie called *First Man* was released, focusing on Neil Armstrong and his trip to the Moon.

The Moon landing is also featured in many video

games. Several have included recreations of the original televised footage. *Lego Marvel Super Heroes*, *Kerbal Space Program* and *Command & Conquer: Yuri's Revenge* all reference the event.

Though the footage from the Moon landing is five decades old, it remains an important part of modern culture. This is because it continues to appear in new art, television and video games. As new artists reuse and manipulate the footage, they add their own spin onto the way it exists in the world.

The first time the world saw Apollo 11's television broadcast, it represented a huge technological leap for humanity. Not only were men walking on the

Moon, but they were also broadcasting it live. Modern viewers see the video differently. They notice the poor quality of the footage, the crackly audio, the blurry pictures. This changes the way they interpret what they see. Modern viewers also realise that many advances in space occurred after the first Moon landing. Today space agencies are preparing for new trips to the Moon. They are also working towards a mission to Mars.

As NASA and other space agencies work to explore new frontiers in space, the importance of the first Moon landing will not be diminished. The video footage of the landing, and the impression it made on a generation of worldwide viewers, will continue to hold a significant place in history.

Timeline

4 October 1957

Scientists in the Soviet Union launch the first human-made satellite into Earth's orbit. It is called *Sputnik*.

12 April 1961

Soviet cosmonaut Yuri Gagarin becomes the first human to fly in space. He orbits Earth once.

20 February 1962

John Glenn becomes the first American to orbit Earth.

22 November 1963

Lee Harvey Oswald assassinates President John F. Kennedy in Dallas, Texas, USA.

May 1961–May 1963

NASA launches six missions during Project Mercury.

5 May 1961

Alan Shepard becomes the first American to fly in space. His mission lasts a little more than 15 minutes.

25 May 1961

President John F. Kennedy makes a speech to a joint session of Congress in which he says, "I believe that this nation should commit itself to achieving the goal, before this decade is out, of landing a man on the Moon and returning him safely to Earth."

March 1965–November 1966

NASA launches 10 missions during Project Gemini.

3 February 1966

Soviet spacecraft *Luna 9* makes an unmanned lunar landing and transmits images of the Moon's surface back to Earth.

Timeline

27 January 1967

The crew of Apollo 1 dies in a fire during a launch rehearsal.

October 1968–December 1972

NASA launches 11 missions during Project Apollo.

21 July 1969

Eagle leaves the Moon and reunites with the command module, *Columbia*.

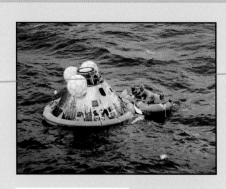

24 July 1969

Apollo 11 crew safely splash into the Pacific Ocean.

16 July 1969

Apollo 11 launches from Cape Canaveral, Florida, USA.

20 July 1969

Apollo 11's lunar module, *Eagle*, lands on the Moon. Neil Armstrong and Buzz Aldrin take their first moonwalk. It is broadcast around the world.

August 1969

WH Auden publishes a poem called "Moon Landing".

1 August 1981

MTV's first moments on television show uses footage from Apollo 11.

2018

The movie *First Man* uses footage of the Apollo 11 launch and Moon landing.

Glossary

broadcast to send out a programme over the radio or on television

command module the part of a spacecraft that can support human life during launch and re-entry

console a cabinet or desk containing the equipment necessary for a certain job

dock to join two spacecraft in space

gravity the force that attracts objects towards Earth or other bodies with mass

hoax a trick to make people believe something that is not real

lunar module the part of a spacecraft that can be used to fly down to the Moon, land and take off again

orbit the path an object takes as it moves around a celestial body

satellite a human-made object placed in orbit around the Earth, Moon or other celestial body

tripod a three-legged stand used to hold a camera

watt unit used to measure electrical power

Find out more

Books

The First Moon Landing (Graphic History),
Thomas Anderson (Raintree, 2011)

*The Race to Space: From the Launch of Sputnik
to the Moon Landing,* Clive Gifford (Words and
Pictures, 2019)

Who Travelled to the Moon? (Primary Source
Detectives), Neil Morris (Raintree, 2015)

Websites

Experience the Apollo 11 Lunar Landing:
www.firstmenonthemoon.com

**NASA. Find out how the landing sites
were selected:**
www.nasa.gov/feature/50-years-ago-lunar-
landing-sites-selected

**NASA. Watch the footage of the landing
on the Moon:**
www.nasa.gov/mission_pages/apollo/
apollo11.html

Comprehension questions

Consider the challenges facing
NASA in its quest to take a
human to the Moon. How do
you think televising each step
towards the Moon landing
helped the agency? How did it
make things more difficult?

How did television news stations
play up NASA launches? What
did they do to enhance their
broadcasts? Use evidence from
the text to support your answer.

One reason NASA televised the
Moon landing was to provide
people with evidence that it had
actually occurred. How have
people used the footage from the
Moon landing to argue that it
was a hoax?

Source notes

p. 4, "Houston...Tranquility Base here..." "Historic Mission Control," *SpaceCenter.org*, https://spacecenter.org/attractions/nasa-tram-tour/historic-mission-control/ Accessed April 20, 2018

p. 4, "Roger, Tranquility..." Ibid.

p. 11, "Man, we're getting..." "Man Walks on Another World," *NationalGeographic.com*, http://ngm.nationalgeographic.com/print/1969/12/moon-landing/astronauts-text Accessed April 20, 2018.

p. 12, "It's almost like a powder..." Ibid.

p. 13, "That's one small step..." Ibid.

p. 14, "Oh, thank you..." "Apollo 11 Part 27, CBS News Coverage of the Moon Walk," August 18, 2010, https://www.youtube.com/watch?v=XisDvCTww4M Accessed April 20, 2018.

pp. 20–21, "I believe that this nation..." "The Moon Decision," *AirandSpace.si.edu*, https://airandspace.si.edu/exhibitions/apollo-to-the-moon/online/racing-to-space/moon-decision.cfm Accessed April 20, 2018.

p. 21, "Go, baby!" John Glenn Launch, Walter Cronkite 'Go, Baby!' Live on TV, CBS, February 20, 1962," *Youtube.com*, November 5, 2011, https://www.youtube.com/watch?v=GVB5dg7XX_g Accessed April 20, 2018.

p. 24, "I feel like a million dollars!" Bob Evans, "To Swim in Space: The World's First Spacewalk (Part 2)." *AmericaSpace.com*, http://www.americaspace.com/2014/03/09/to-swim-in-space-the-worlds-first-spacewalk-part-2/ Accessed April 20, 2018.

p. 28, "I'm going to hang it..." https://history.nasa.gov/Apollo204/zorn/grissom.htm Accessed April 20, 2018.

p. 34, "Oh boy..." "Launch of Apollo 11 (CBS)," *Youtube.com*, April 1, 2010, https://www.youtube.com/watch?v=TmHABUfjYPI Accessed April 20, 2018.

p. 36, "... a most historic event..." Steve Knoll, "First Man on the Moon Has the Networks in Orbit," *Variety.com*, July 16, 1969, http://variety.com/1969/biz/news/first-man-on-the-moon-has-tv-networks-in-orbit-1201342630/ Accessed April 20, 2018.

p. 39, "Program alarm..." "CBS Coverage of Apollo 11 Lunar Landing," *Youtube.com*, July 17, 2014, https://www.youtube.com/watch?v=E96EPhqT-ds Accessed April 30, 2018.

p. 39, "We're go on that alarm. ..." Ibid.

p. 40, "You're GO for landing..." Andrew Chaikin, *A Man on the Moon*. New York: Penguin, 2007, p. 196.

p. 41, "You guys are getting..." Ibid., p. 204.

p. 43, "LIVE FROM THE SURFACE ..." CBS Coverage of Apollo 11 Lunar Landing, "*Youtube.com*, July 17, 2014, https://www.youtube.com/watch?v=E96EPhqT-ds Accessed April 20, 2018.

pp. 47–48, ""This is the greatest week..." "Apollo 11 and the World." *AirandSpace.Si.edu*, July 15, 2009, https://airandspace.si.edu/stories/editorial/apollo-11-and-world Accessed April 20, 2018.

p. 48, "Americans reached out ..." "Man on the Moon: 45 Years Later, Remembering Apollo 11," *USNews.com*, July 21, 2014, https://www.usnews.com/news/articles/2014/07/21/man-on-the-moon-45-years-later-remembering-the-apollo-11-moon-landing Accessed April 20, 2018.

p. 51, "...expressed doubts..." "Why Do People Persist in Denying the Moon Landings?" *AirandSpace.si.edu*, April 1, 2010 https://airandspace.si.edu/stories/editorial/why-do-people-persist-denying-moon-landings Accessed April 20, 2018.

p. 51, "if people decide..." "Why Do People Persist in Denying the Moon Landings?"

p. 51, "a coward, a liar..." Brandon Griggs, "Could Moon Landings Have Been Faked? Some Still Think So." *CNN.com*, July 17, 2009, Accessed April 10, 2018.

p. 52, "Unsmudged..." W.H. Auden, *Universification.wordpress.com*, https://universification.wordpress.com/2012/11/04/moon-landing-w-h-auden

p. 52, "We thought, 'We're like the guys...'" Madeline Roth, "Ever Wondered Why the VMA Statue is a Moonman?" *MTV.com*, August 27, 2016, http://www.mtv.com/news/2924701/vma-statue-moonman/ Accessed April 20, 2018.

Select bibliography

"The Apollo 1 Tragedy." NASA.gov, Digital, https://nssdc.gsfc.nasa.gov/planetary/lunar/apollo1info.html Accessed February 2, 2018.

Chaikin, Andrew. *A Man on the Moon*. New York: Penguin, 2007.

Kennedy, John F. "Address Before a Joint Session of Congress, May 25, 1961," JFKlibrary.org, Digital, https://www.jfklibrary.org/Asset-Viewer/xzw1gaeeTES6khED14P1Iw.aspx Accessed March 3, 2018.

Lovell, Jim, and Jeffrey Kluger. *Apollo 13*. New York: Houghton Mifflin, 1994.

"Why Do People Persist in Denying the Moon Landings?" AirandSpace.SI.edu, April 1, 2010, Digital 8, https://airandspace.si.edu/stories/editorial/why-do-people-persist-denying-moon-landings Accessed March 4, 2018.

Index

About the author

Rebecca Rissman is an award-winning non-fiction author of more than 300 books. Her work has been praised by *School Library Journal*, *Booklist*, *Creative Child Magazine* and *Learning* magazine. Rissman especially enjoys writing about American history, aeronautics and women. She lives in Chicago, Illinois, USA, with her husband and two daughters.